The Victoria Line

A SHORT HISTORY

by

M. A. C. Horne

1988
Published by Douglas Rose
35 Summers Lane, North Finchley, London N12 0PE

but

Distributed by Nebulous Books
12 Raven Square, Alton, Hampshire GU34 2LL

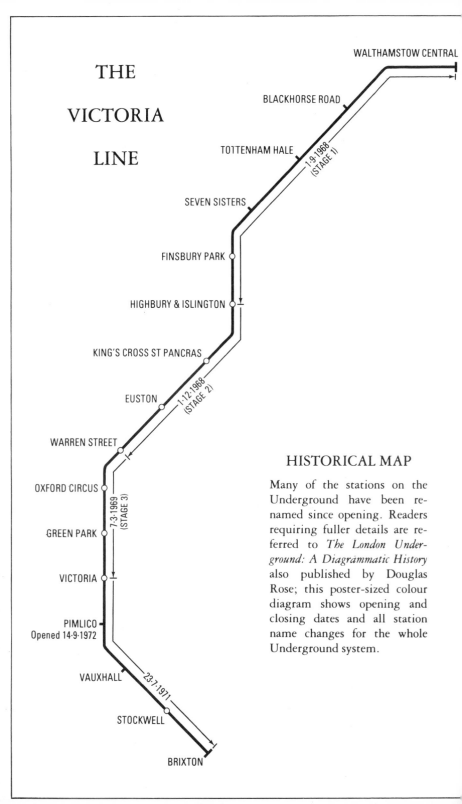

THE

VICTORIA

LINE

WALTHAMSTOW CENTRAL

BLACKHORSE ROAD

TOTTENHAM HALE

1·9·1968
(STAGE 1)

SEVEN SISTERS

FINSBURY PARK

HIGHBURY & ISLINGTON

KING'S CROSS ST PANCRAS

EUSTON

1·12·1968
(STAGE 2)

WARREN STREET

OXFORD CIRCUS

7·3·1969
(STAGE 3)

GREEN PARK

VICTORIA

PIMLICO
Opened 14·9·1972

VAUXHALL

23·7·1971

STOCKWELL

BRIXTON

HISTORICAL MAP

Many of the stations on the Underground have been re-named since opening. Readers requiring fuller details are referred to *The London Underground: A Diagrammatic History* also published by Douglas Rose; this poster-sized colour diagram shows opening and closing dates and all station name changes for the whole Underground system.

Part of the experimental section of Victoria Line tunnel north of Finsbury Park in 1962. This apparently surreal view actually shows a test rig equipped with pitot tubes, and is designed to measure the air velocity created by a test train farther back, where a length of track had been laid. _LTE official photograph_ *

To C. E. L.

The Victoria Line: A Short History
by M. A. C. Horne
ISBN 1 870354 02 8
First published in August 1988
© Copyright M. A. C. Horne

Other short histories in this series by M. A. C. Horne
THE NORTHERN LINE
THE CENTRAL LINE

The author and publisher wish to acknowledge the assistance of
George Jasieniecki, Peter Bancroft, Suzanne Tagg, and
particularly to Jonathan Roberts and John Liffen.

Photographs marked with an asterisk (*) are reproduced
by kind permission of the London Transport Museum.
Copy prints may be ordered from the Museum's Photo
Library.

The text in this book has been set in
Linotype Garamond No. 3 10/11pt and 8/8½pt,
with appropriate italic and small caps,
on a Linotron 202.

Typeset by Douglas Rose, London N12 0PE.
Cover design by Art Attack, London SW9 6AR,
from an idea by M. A. C. Horne.
Printed by Printline (Offset) Limited, London EC1R 4RB.

THE VICTORIA LINE, though twenty years old, is the most recent completely new addition to London's Underground. It is remarkable in being the Underground's only line to be operated by automatically driven trains, and the only one to operate below ground throughout its 13·3 miles (21·3km). Perhaps more surprising is that it was the first new railway across central London for over 60 years.

The main portion of the new line ran from Walthamstow Central to Victoria, although it was not all completed at the same time and opened in stages. The first stage was from Walthamstow to Highbury, the second one extended it to Warren Street and the third stage to Victoria (Brixton came later). It was not felt appropriate to have an opening ceremony until the line reached Victoria, and it was at 11:30am on 7th March 1969 that Her Majesty Queen Elizabeth II pressed the twin start buttons in the cab of one of the new Victoria Line trains and 'drove' it automatically between Green Park and Oxford Circus stations (for some years this car – 3052 – carried a small plaque commemorating the event). At 3pm the public gained their first access to London's latest tube. They liked it, and have flocked to it ever since.

This book explains how the need for the new line was first perceived, how plans developed, and how the Victoria Line has been built and operated. There have of course been many proposals for tube railways across central London since the Edwardian era of tube construction; the main criterion used by the author has been to consider those schemes based on a railway linking Finsbury Park with Victoria, and Victoria with south London.

Although post-war Britain was the stage upon which the Victoria Line developments were enacted, the scene was really set in the pre-war world of 1933. During the course of that year the London Passenger Transport Board (LPTB) was formed and from 1st July the LPTB had the responsibility of running all the Underground lines, bus and tramway services in a huge area in and around London.

The LPTB inherited both a deep-level system of tube railways, and a largely separate network of shallow tunnel and open air railways. The 'surface' system consisted of the substantially Victorian origin Circle, District and Metropolitan Lines, largely bordering or operating outside the central area. The tube lines were a little more recent and had been built as relatively short, high-capacity, frequent-interval lines which mainly criss-crossed central London. After the First World War the emphasis of development was to utilize the surplus capacity of the increasingly efficient tubes by projecting them outwards into the suburbs-to-be, generating new traffic as they went. The desire for building new central

Her Majesty the Queen at the Line's opening ceremony obtaining a 5d ticket from a ticket-and-change machine for use in one of the automatic barriers. The first Royal sixpence declined to co-operate and another had to be obtained. *LTB official photograph*

London tubes thus diminished.

This general trend continued until the Second World War, and then the 'Green Belt' philosophy, expenditure and materials restrictions, and the extension of car ownership, all stifled further outward development. But the demand for in-town services did continue to rise, fuelled by central London office development, increasing road congestion and the growth of longer-distance commuting on the main line railways. Inevitably this began to place some of the central area stations under considerable pressure – the time was ripe for considering once more the building of new tube lines across central London.

A feature of the 1933 arrangements was that both the Board and the main line railways were party to a statutory revenue pooling scheme for local passenger services provided within the LPT Area. The Pool was administered by a Standing Joint Committee of the Board and the railway companies, but the Board was by far the most influential partner. The revenue pool meant that the jealousies and rivalries of the 1920s were inappropriate, and that co-operation (increasing the total revenue of the Pool) benefited all the partners. Within months a large-scale programme of new investment was being developed which became the 1935–40 New Works

Programme. A result of this administrative arrangement was that the new works, in addition to extension of several tube lines, involved the electrification of some main line branches with Underground trains taking over the passenger services.

In 1936 an LPTB team visited New York where they were much taken with that city's rapid transit system where the railway lines carrying the 'all stations' services were often duplicated by 'express' lines with occasional facilities for interchange between the two. This both increased carrying capacity and made for a quicker and more attractive journey to and from the outer areas.

At about the same time it began to be accepted that despite modernization work London's existing central area lines could be placed under severe pressure by all the additional traffic from the proposed outer London extensions. In the light of the New York visit 'express' tubes were suggested, one paralleling the Central Line between Liverpool Street and Marble Arch, and another paralleling the Northern Line between Archway and Tottenham Court Road. Connections would be made to the existing tracks at each end. Another proposal was for a new express tube from Victoria via Bond Street and Baker Street to Finchley Road and the Metropolitan Line, with interconnections with the Bakerloo Line at Baker Street.

In the following year, 1937, the LPTB's General Manager (Railways) put forward tentative proposals for a further programme of works, to be built between 1940 and 1950. The man concerned was John Pattinson Thomas, who had been a major influence in the drafting of the 1935–40 New Works Programme. He adopted a consistent approach, and again planned to incorporate several branch lines of the London & North Eastern Railway (LNER) into the Underground. Thomas envisaged electrification of the Palace Gates, Enfield Town and Chingford branches to London Transport standards and plugging them into a new tube railway heading towards Finsbury Park (a similar process was then taking place with the 1935–40 Central Line eastern extensions to Hainault and Ongar). From this point it was thought that part of the service could operate to the City via the existing Northern City tube, on which there was spare capacity beyond that required for the proposed new Northern Line services to Alexandra Palace and High Barnet. The balance of the service would continue south-westwards in a new express tube towards Victoria via the West End.

The express tube was in essence the proposed Archway to Tottenham Court Road line, diverted at the northern end to Finsbury Park and extended at the southern end. Intermediate stations were speculatively suggested at Camden Town, Tottenham Court Road and Piccadilly Circus. The objective of this alignment was to divert

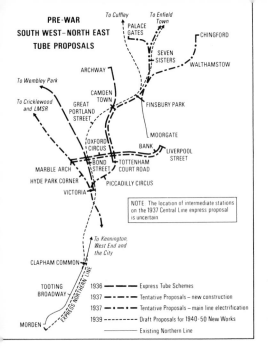

PRE-WAR
SOUTH WEST–NORTH EAST
TUBE PROPOSALS

To Cuffley   To Enfield Town
PALACE GATES
CHINGFORD
SEVEN SISTERS
WALTHAMSTOW
ARCHWAY
To Wembley Park
CAMDEN TOWN
To Cricklewood and LMSR
GREAT PORTLAND STREET
FINSBURY PARK
MOORGATE
OXFORD CIRCUS
BANK
LIVERPOOL STREET
BOND STREET
TOTTENHAM COURT ROAD
MARBLE ARCH
HYDE PARK CORNER
PICCADILLY CIRCUS
VICTORIA

NOTE: The location of intermediate stations on the 1937 Central Line express proposal is uncertain

To Kennington, West End and the City
CLAPHAM COMMON
TOOTING BROADWAY
MORDEN

1936 ━━━ Express Tube Schemes
1937 ━·━·━ Tentative Proposals – new construction
1937 ━·━·━ Tentative Proposals – main line electrification
1939 ------- Draft Proposals for 1940-50 New Works
━━━ Existing Northern Line

EXPRESS NORTHERN LINE

a proportion of existing traffic away from two of the busiest sections of the Underground, on the Piccadilly and Northern Lines. The line would also divert passengers from Liverpool Street and the Central Line, heavily used in the central area and still deemed to need its own 'relief' express tube once its eastern extensions opened.

Another component of Thomas's plan was a revival of an old idea – a tube railway from Cricklewood to Victoria via the Edgware Road, Marble Arch and Hyde Park Corner (which effectively superseded the Victoria–Baker Street 1936 scheme). This time a large-diameter tube was contemplated, with a view to connecting with the St Pancras main line of the London, Midland & Scottish Railway. A St Albans–Victoria service using main line size electric trains might eventually be extended south of Victoria in new tunnels, possibly via Oval, to an unspecified southern terminus; this would relieve the hard-pressed Morden extension of the Northern Line and certain Southern Railway services. Stations allowing of 10 or 12-car trains were now talked of whereas existing standards were for 8 or 9-cars.

These schemes were highly speculative but are the first indications of the general transport corridors along which it was felt necessary to improve services by means of completely new construction. During subsequent government discussions in mid-1938 the proposals were illustrated to show the nature of the developments required. These were still broadly similar to Thomas's 1937 proposals and included the Finsbury Park to Victoria tube, although the northern termini were now unspecified. The Chingford and Edmonton branches were listed separately among other lines to be electrified (by the LNER), and no specific link with the new tube was indicated.

The government's support was vital, and the relevant Assistant Secretary proved very supportive in putting forward the Board's proposals to his Minister. This set out a case for further expenditure of the order of £50–£60 million on London's transport facilities, a programme at least as large (at 1940s prices) as the 1935–40 New Works. However, the financial background against which the

8

proposals were considered was not favourable. The cost of the 1935–40 programme had been underestimated and various modifications, and inflation, had taken their toll. The Board had insufficient spare cash to meet the additional costs and the LNER was already in serious financial difficulty. Some aspects of the programme were only retained because of contractual or legal obligations, and critical eyes continued to look at areas where substantial economies could be made. This was hardly the best position from which to embark on building new railways.

It was not until 7th January 1939 that the Standing Joint Committee of the LPTB and main line companies called for a report, "offering a preliminary view of requirements for new transport facilities for London in the following ten years", in other words ideas for another 'New Works' programme. The report was signed on 31st August, three days before war against Germany was declared, and was not the most pressing matter in hand at the time. Nevertheless it does suggest a further development of ideas.

The 1939 plan reviewed the existing sections of overcrowded railway but was now markedly unenthusiastic about a simple duplication of railway lines (except at the south end of the Northern Line) on the grounds that it would only be of value during the peak hours. To justify such relief facilities new railways would also have to serve new areas in order to build up a base traffic of their own. Two major railway schemes were included. Electrification of the Midland and the High Wycombe–Marylebone main lines was one, with trains projected via a new tube through the West End to Victoria (clearly superseding the 'Cricklewood' tube proposal of 1937).

The Victoria to Finsbury Park proposal was also developed further. Stage 1 envisaged duplicating the Northern Line between Morden and Clapham Common, but on a shorter alignment. From Clapham Common a new line would then run towards a temporary terminus at Victoria. With the Northern Line trains running express through the new tube from Morden to Clapham Common, calling only at Tooting Broadway, and the existing 'all stations' service from Morden diverging from the old route at Clapham Common and running express to Victoria, passengers could interchange as necessary at Clapham Common. The combination of both lines would significantly speed up the journey time from the outer reaches and ease overcrowding.

Stage 2 of the new line was similar in principle to the earlier Victoria–Finsbury Park proposal but on a slightly different route via Green Park, Bond Street, Great Portland Street, thence to Camden Town and express to Finsbury Park. This reflected a preference for avoiding direct duplication of the Northern Line.

Stage 3 would see the new line merge north of Finsbury Park with an extension from the low-level Northern City Line terminus and continue in tube beneath the LNER line to Bowes Road, replacing the LNER stations at Harringay, Hornsey and Wood Green. The line would then surface and run on electrified LNER tracks towards Cuffley. North of Finsbury Park, junctions (similar to those at Camden Town on the Northern Line) would also allow part of the joint service to proceed in tube towards Seven Sisters and thence to Enfield Town.

The Second World War severely reduced planning work on any expansion of the Underground: more urgent tasks took precedence. However, wartime did contrive certain opportunities. In October 1940 the government and LPTB discussed building a number of deep-level air-raid shelters with the possibility that after the war they could be incorporated into tube railway expansion schemes. The Board stated that they had only rough and not fully developed schemes in mind. It was therefore agreed that the shelter tunnels would be placed parallel with existing lines, not on speculative alignments of brand-new tubes. This would reduce the cost of duplicating overcrowded sections of railway after the war, should the need arise. The proposals inevitably rekindled some of the pre-1939 development thinking where simple duplication of lines was favoured. It was perhaps appropriate that J. P. Thomas was hauled back from retirement to run the deep shelter programme.

The sections immediately thought worthy of duplication were Camden Town to Tottenham Court Road, Kennington to Balham and Bank to Holborn. Shelters were therefore considered at Mornington Crescent, Warren Street, Goodge Street, Oval, Stockwell, Clapham North, Clapham Common, Clapham South, St Paul's and Chancery Lane, a total of ten. Later on, Mornington Crescent and Warren Street shelters were dropped in favour of others at Belsize Park and Camden Town; Oval was started but not completed and St Paul's was not built. In the context of late 1930s plans some shelters were conveniently sited for a future South London–Victoria–Finsbury Park tube.

The next hint at future developments appears to have been in 1943 in a document produced by the Ministry of War Transport. This appeared under the hand of Colonel Alan Mount, Chief Inspecting Officer of Railways to the Ministry, and sets out for consideration the development of railway facilities in post-war Britain.

Colonel Mount favoured the 'Finsbury Park to Victoria' tube, with a southern alignment continuing on to meet and then follow the 'express' Northern Line scheme to Morden (but now with a possible extension to Cheam); north of Finsbury Park the preferred alignment remained towards Bowes Park and thence (unspecifically) on to the LNER system. However, the central London alignment reverted to the route via Tottenham Court Road, and the Great Portland Street objective appears to have been lost. While this is not explained, the other main work was a return to the Victoria–Cricklewood scheme (rather than the more ambitious 1939 proposals) and this effectively duplicated much of the Victoria–Great Portland Street route.

A development from the 1939 scheme (and the statements made in connection with the deep shelters in 1940) now acknowledged that the overcrowding on the Northern Line actually began north of Camden Town. An ambitious scheme was thus suggested whereby that line would be entirely duplicated between Golders Green and Morden by an express tube. The existence of the wartime shelter tunnels may have swayed Mount's thinking. If this option were pursued then it was proposed that the separate Finsbury Park–Tottenham Court Road–Victoria–Morden proposal would be curtailed at an exchange station at Clapham Common. An express tube following the Central Line west of Liverpool Street was still being considered, though now extended farther west, to Wood Lane.

Equally optimistic planning, on an even grander scale, was unveiled in 1943 as the County of London Plan, devised by J. H. Forshaw, Superintending Architect to the London County Council, assisted by Sir Patrick Abercrombie. It followed the prevailing ideology among architects by proposing the drastic rebuilding of much of London, both to group activities by zone and to cope with traffic growth. Major expansion of the Underground was not favoured, interconnection between the main line railways being preferred. Extensive proposals were made for a scheme of interlinked loop tunnels under central London for main line trains; these satisfied the current desire to replace the Thames railway bridges so abhorrent to the architectural profession.

While the County of London Plan gave a psychological boost to a city still at war, its practicability was less inspiring during postwar austerity. Other, more modest, plans soon superseded the 1943 ideas. But one of the Plan's more useful suggestions had already been acted upon. It had proposed the setting up of a committee specifically to look at the railway implications of the plan and to produce detailed proposals. The recommendation was adopted and the Railway (London Plan) Committee was appointed on 22nd February 1944.

The Committee was a substantially railway-orientated body which included Colonel (and by now Sir) Alan Mount and representatives of the LPTB and the main line companies. In its first report of 21st January 1946 a somewhat jaundiced view of the proposals

11

for the demise of the railway bridges was taken and recommendations were formulated which bore an interesting resemblance to the Ministry's 1943 plan. The Finsbury Park to Victoria link survived, albeit somewhat adjusted, as ROUTE 8 in the proposed plan.

Major changes between the 1946 plan and its forebears included dropping the Central Line express tube in favour of independent east–west tubes and diversion of the Cricklewood tube away from Victoria towards Charing Cross, Cannon Street and London Bridge. The duplication of the Northern Line from at least Camden Town to Morden was allowed for, with the section from Kennington to Tooting regarded as urgent.

With wholesale duplication of the Northern Line now being suggested, the central London routeing of the Victoria–Finsbury Park proposal (ROUTE 8) no longer needed to do the same thing, and it resulted in the line being shifted westwards, to tackle different traffic flows. These were principally some of the most heavily used existing connections, such as the Victoria–Euston and Victoria–King's Cross traffics. Similarly, journeys from Victoria to Mayfair and Oxford Street were circuitous and it was desired to reduce the pressure of traffic at Victoria (District Line) station and interchange traffic at Tottenham Court Road and Leicester Square. The revised central London route therefore became King's Cross, Euston, Bond Street and Hyde Park Corner to Victoria.

North of Finsbury Park, ROUTE 8 remained aimed towards Bowes Park to join the LNER with a view to running over newly electrified tracks northwards (the actual limit of running was still not precisely defined). South of Victoria ROUTE 8 no longer needed to make a link at Kennington and a route to East Croydon via Vauxhall, Stockwell (Northern Line interchange), Brixton, Streatham and Norbury was proposed instead, the line running at surface level beyond Norbury. The section from Croydon to Finsbury Park was to be 14 miles (22·4km) long and the expected cost was then £24 million. It had been recommended that the new tube be built to a new standard which allowed for 17ft (5·2m) diameter tunnels (main line size) with platforms 16ft (4·9m) wide and 650ft (198m) long – nearly double the length of existing platforms, and long enough for 12-car trains. The numerous schemes recommended by the Committee were divided into four levels of priority, and ROUTE 8 was given the status of a first priority work "to meet immediate traffic requirements".

It might be mentioned that against this planning background the Standing Joint Committee of the Board and main line railways still existed and met several times during 1946 to look at post-war investment priorities. Almost perversely it was slow to contribute to the debate on the London Plan tubes, although it did eventually acknowledge the usefulness of ROUTE 8, but thought the southern end could be turned west as an express railway serving the Osterley World Fair in 1951, and thence London Airport (Heathrow).

In contrast, the LPTB, even in its final year of existence, adopted a very positive approach. It enthusiastically evaluated the various prevailing schemes, and by February 1947 had put together a detailed draft plan largely based on the London Plan Committee's proposals. ROUTE 8 was favoured, but in a modified form which was termed SCHEME D. In central London a revised route took the line via Green Park and Oxford Circus stations, instead of Hyde Park Corner and Bond Street. This was felt a substantially better option which allowed same-level interchange with the Bakerloo Line at Oxford Circus. This station was quite inadequate for the prevailing traffic and had an inefficient and congested layout – so much so that it had previously been thought to make the addition of a new line with same-level interchange impracticably difficult. Nevertheless a scheme had been devised although it was only possible if SCHEME D was of conventional 12ft (3·8m) bore and not the 17ft (5·2m) bore intended for ROUTE 8; almost total reconstruction of the station was also required.

To the south of Victoria, SCHEME D was not greatly dissimilar to ROUTE 8 except that it was proposed to extend to West (instead of East) Croydon and thence beyond at surface level to South Croydon where the line would bifurcate to branches at Coulsdon North and Sanderstead.

North of Finsbury Park, SCHEME D was quite different from ROUTE 8 and reflected a complete rethink in the manner of improving the LNER branch and main line services. It was proposed to extend the new tube line north-eastwards to Seven Sisters where it would split into two branches, one to Hoe Street (in Walthamstow) and the other to Tottenham Hale from which point trains would be projected at surface level to Waltham Cross. One of the main objectives in doing this was to intercept nearly all radial and orbital lines in that sector of London. Thus interchanges with the Chingford branch would be made at Hoe Street, Tottenham loop line at Blackhorse Road, Waltham Cross line by direct service, Enfield Town and Palace Gates branches at Seven Sisters, Piccadilly Line at Manor House, LNER main line and Northern Line at Finsbury Park and the North London Line at Barnsbury. A 36 trains per hour maximum service was proposed on the main section of the line with 18 trains per hour on the branches (except north of Tottenham Hale where six were proposed).

While London Transport was examining its response to the Working Party's report of 1946 there were major administrative changes looming. During the war both the LPTB and main line

13

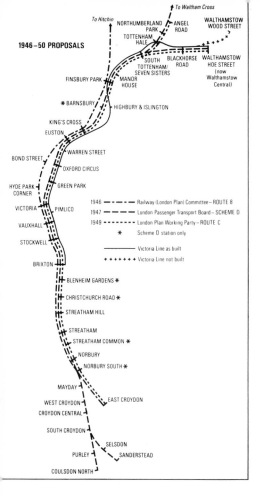

1946–50 PROPOSALS

To Waltham Cross

To Hitchin

NORTHUMBERLAND PARK — ANGEL ROAD

WALTHAMSTOW WOOD STREET

TOTTENHAM HALE

SOUTH TOTTENHAM/ SEVEN SISTERS — BLACKHORSE ROAD — WALTHAMSTOW HOE STREET (now Walthamstow Central)

FINSBURY PARK — MANOR HOUSE

* BARNSBURY — HIGHBURY & ISLINGTON

KING'S CROSS
EUSTON
WARREN STREET
BOND STREET
OXFORD CIRCUS
HYDE PARK CORNER — GREEN PARK
VICTORIA — PIMLICO
VAUXHALL
STOCKWELL
BRIXTON
BLENHEIM GARDENS *
CHRISTCHURCH ROAD *
STREATHAM HILL
STREATHAM
STREATHAM COMMON *
NORBURY
NORBURY SOUTH *
MAYDAY
WEST CROYDON — EAST CROYDON
CROYDON CENTRAL
SOUTH CROYDON
SELSDON
PURLEY — SANDERSTEAD
COULSDON NORTH

1946 — · — · — Railway (London Plan) Committee – ROUTE 8
1947 ————— London Passenger Transport Board – SCHEME D
1949 · · · · · · · London Plan Working Party – ROUTE C
    *   Scheme D station only
    ———————   Victoria Line as built
    + + + + + +   Victoria Line not built

companies had been placed under government control, the link being made by establishing the Railway Executive Committee. This arrangement continued after the war, during which time the new government decided upon the nationalization of inland public transport. The system was to be vested in a body called the British Transport Commission (BTC), which effectively superseded the Railway Executive Committee. Separate statutory executive bodies were established in order to run the various arms of the business. Ironically, common ownership spelled the end of the London revenue pool and the manner of the planning process which went with it, the new executives largely working in isolation. On 1st January 1948 the London Passenger Transport Board thus passed to the London Transport Executive (LT), while the main line railways passed to the Railway Executive (British Railways – BR).

The political and administrative upheaval inevitably clouded the issue of future planning. As a result, on 1st April 1948, the Chairman of the Commission advised the Minister of Transport that he had set up a working party to examine the proposals of the Railway (London Plan) Committee "in the light of the latest economic and other developments". Its report was published in 1949.

It was inevitable that the new Working Party would take on board the detailed examinations already made, and not perhaps surprising that it came out strongly in favour of building ROUTE 8, but incorporating nearly all the modifications already suggested by London Transport in their SCHEME D. The result was a specific proposal to build a new 12ft diameter tube railway referred to as ROUTE C. The Working Party saw no reason to deviate from the London Plan proposals at the Croydon end, so favoured East Croydon as the terminus. At the northern end of the line the Working Party preferred a tube line from Seven Sisters northwards

14

only as far as an interchange with the BR Eastern Region at Angel Road, on the Waltham Cross line; this line was in any case the subject of a separate electrification proposal.

An optional branch line from Seven Sisters to Walthamstow Hoe Street via Blackhorse Road was given the status "possibly desirable". ROUTE C as a whole was described as "a most important traffic route" and was included among the four most urgent schemes to proceed.

The London Plan Working Party continued to meet under BTC auspices after the publication of their main report and made observations as appropriate. The grand schemes formulated in the 1940s gradually evaporated in the light of post-war reality where cash and materials shortages prevented even the proper maintenance of existing facilities. The prospect of massive new investment on additional schemes took on an air of an improbable dream. Nearly all the proposals were eventually dropped; only the most pressing were kept alive, these being ROUTE C (north-east London to Croydon) and ROUTE D (a south-west to north-east London scheme via Victoria and Fleet Street).

By 1951 the Working Party had concluded that the northern end of ROUTE C should only serve the proposed 'branch' service to Blackhorse Road and Walthamstow. By diverting this branch via Tottenham Hale it was possible to retain interchange with the Waltham Cross line, though by escalators rather than by a direct service. Walthamstow was now felt to be best served by a station in the town centre at Hoe Street, and with a same-level interchange with the Chingford branch service at Wood Street station. By this time it had become the long-term objective to electrify the Eastern Region suburban services to Enfield and Chingford (though detailed proposals were not made until 1955). The Finsbury Park to Victoria routeing remained substantially unchanged.

South of Victoria the ultimate objective for ROUTE C had been Croydon, and the alignment via Vauxhall, Stockwell, Brixton, Streatham and Norbury remained as intended earlier. In Croydon itself the alignment presented problems. BR Southern Region planners were most anxious that the line reached East Croydon to provide interchange with the main line to Brighton, which would mean that ROUTE C would miss Croydon town centre unless severe curves were put in. The solution was to pursue the earlier thinking about dividing the end of the line, with one branch from West Croydon to East Croydon and the other from West Croydon to the town centre and South Croydon; a possible depot site was examined between Selsdon and Sanderstead.

For the next couple of years considerable work took place on detailed planning and in reconciling the conflicting factors dictating the Lea Valley routeing. During this time LT arranged for an aerial survey of this route (and two others) to be undertaken preparatory to full scale engineering surveys. In 1953 the Minister of Transport and Civil Aviation announced that he accepted ROUTE C as a first priority work, to be undertaken when circumstances permitted, but there was no hint as to when this might be (other than not soon). By this time the likelihood of other new works had further receded, and several of the uncompleted Northern Line pre-war new works had been officially cancelled. None of this could have been particularly encouraging to those pressing for the new tube line, and it is clear that the inexorable process of planning perhaps lacked vigour.

By 1954, with government acceptance of the scheme in principle, and with the routeing of the line north of Victoria now settled, the BTC decided to seek parliamentary powers to construct the Victoria–Walthamstow section in their Bill of that year – the principal powers were therefore enshrined in the British Transport Commission Act 1955. The terminal alignment at Victoria suited future extension either towards Croydon or Chelsea and Fulham. A ROUTE C station at Manor House was abandoned because of anticipated difficulties in staging the work, and the station risked overloading the in-town section of the new line.

The parliamentary process undoubtedly transformed ROUTE C from what could have been construed simply as a planners' dream into a scheme perceived as likely to be built. Indeed, it was not then long before the proposed line acquired a name – the Victoria Line – first mentioned tentatively in public in December 1955 and, in the absence of anything better, it stuck.

But the passing of an Act of Parliament, whilst a milestone, in no way committed the BTC to build a new railway. The problem was how to finance the line. Prior to 1948 money was usually provided by private investors, although the diminishing financial attractiveness of railways had latterly caused governments either to guarantee interest or lend some of the money at attractive rates in order to get important facilities built. Nationalized transport was not able to do this, money had either to be provided from within the impoverished BTC or by the government, and then only by way of a loan upon which interest was charged.

It is worth looking at the financial forecasts of the mid nineteen-fifties to see quite where the sticking point arose. It was estimated that the Victoria Line would cost £50 million to build. This represented works and equipment costs of £40 million, with £2 million for land and easements, £4 million for rolling stock and £4 million for plant and overheads. At the prevailing fixed interest rate of 4 per cent, the annual interest charges to the Commission (in practice, to London Transport) would be some £2 million.

It was estimated that the line would cost a million pounds a year to run. While traffic receipts were thought likely to exceed running costs by some £350,000 a year, it was realized that much of the traffic carried on the new line would be existing traffic which had diverted, so that over the system as a whole there would be a net deficit of about £250,000 a year. Added to the interest charges the line would therefore require some £2·25 million to be found. In the context of annual fares revenue of £100 million for all the BTC's London area services, this represented a fares increase of 2¼ per cent (it may be recalled that for charging purposes the London area was considered a discrete unit where equal fares applied on all the BTC's services).

The issue was therefore very much a social one. The new tube was likely to be of considerable benefit to London. It would open up new areas to Underground travel, speed up numerous cross London journeys (especially between some main line termini), considerably ease congestion at many stations and overcrowded sections of line, and also relieve a certain amount of street congestion. The idea of charging its net revenue loss against fares was not liked within the BTC or London Transport, but the government were not prepared to make a capital grant towards tube railway construction from public funds although, even then, such grants were made for road construction. Although the exact figures varied from year to year the impasse on financing the new line remained for a further six years, and it had already taken nine years to transform a 'high priority' proposal (and not a new one either) into an Act of Parliament.

In 1959 the London Travel Committee examined the Victoria Line against a background of travel improvements of comparable costs; the Victoria Line came out exceedingly well. The Committee reported to the Minister that the "... Victoria Line as it is at present planned should be authorized forthwith and construction put in hand as quickly as possible". This did not happen.

Meanwhile, London Transport had decided to make a detailed study of the latest tunnelling techniques to take account of the significant improvements which had been made since its last involvement with extensive railway tunnelling some twenty years previously.

A particular technical advance had been made in the form of a machine called the 'drum digger'. This had just been used on a remarkable 19-mile (30km) long, 8ft 6ins (2·6m) internal diameter tunnel built by the Metropolitan Water Board between Hampton and the Lea Valley reservoirs. The machine consisted of the usual cylindrical shield which was pushed forward by hydraulic rams, the space behind each thrust then being lined by the tunnel lining segments. At the leading edge of the shield was erected a rotating, circular framework to which cutting teeth were fixed. In turn, the cutting framework was attached to a rotating drum, somewhat smaller than the surrounding shield, and through the centre of which the clay spoil tumbled to be carried away by conveyor to portable skips. A maximum tunnelling speed of 400 feet (120m) per week had been achieved and a scaled-up drum digger appeared to suit the Victoria Line construction.

Tunnel linings, too, had developed substantially since the earliest days of tube railways. These had long been built with cast-iron segmental linings bolted together, with the cavity between the lining and surrounding clay filled under pressure by a cement grouting. This system had a number of disadvantages and in 1949 experiments began into an iron tunnel lining where the segments were expanded against the clay and then locked together by compression of the clay acting on the completed tunnel. There were many problems to be overcome, but in 1958 a 14ft (4·27m) diameter shield-driven tunnel was being built at Belvedere Power Station by the Central Electricity Generating Board, and at LT's expense 20 rings of unbolted iron-lining was erected. This showed that the lining itself was successful and that it was possible to handle and erect the segments satisfactorily.

It had proved expedient while building the eastern extension of the Central Line between 1937 and 1939 to experiment with reinforced concrete linings using pre-cast segments, but otherwise

A Kinnear-Moodie drum digger, fully erected, showing the outer shield and the rotating cutting mechanism which is attached to the internal drum. The aperture 'through which spoil is removed is seen in the centre of the drum.
Science Museum

similar to the traditional iron ones. This type of tunnel had proved slightly more awkward to build, but was cheaper and showed the utility of concrete. For the Victoria Line the cost of concrete tunnels appeared attractive. In any case there were doubts as to whether sufficient iron segments could be made available to furnish the whole of the new line and it was therefore desired to try unbolted, compression-locked concrete segments. Again the Thames–Lea tunnel offered practical experience with such linings and the unbolted concrete segments used there had proved highly successful.

In order to test the new types of tunnelling machines and tunnel linings it was decided to utilize the 1955 parliamentary powers to construct a one mile (1·6km) length of experimental twin tunnel from Finsbury Park to South Tottenham to test the method of building and lining tunnels for the line. Half a million pounds had been put aside by the Commission in 1956 specifically for this work, but this was later doubled. Government authority to build the experimental tunnel was given in 1959 and construction began in January 1960. Working shafts were sunk in Finsbury Park, next to the Eastern Region main line, and at Netherton Road, at the corner of Seven Sisters Road. Once the shafts were sunk tunnel drives were started using drum diggers, the tunnelling teams working towards each other. The intention was that the tunnel drives would meet at a point near Manor House Piccadilly Line station.

The northern section (Manor House to Netherton Road) was built using unbolted cast-iron segments of 12ft 6ins (3·8m) minimum internal diameter, the drum digger shield having an outside diameter of 13ft 1ins (4·0m). The southern section of tunnel (Finsbury Park to Manor House) used a larger drum digger, of 14ft (4·3m) diameter, for use with concrete tunnel linings, which were thicker than the iron ones. The concrete lined tunnels used pre-cast segments which interlocked. Although several thicknesses of segments were tried varying from 4½ to 9 inches (115mm–230mm), 6-inch (150mm) thick segments proved to be the best compromise between the sturdiness required for handling and economy. The internal diameter chosen, and the smooth internal finish of the concrete, was thought likely to significantly reduce the drag on the train due to air resistance, and hence save energy.

By March 1961 one of the bores was complete from Finsbury Park to Manor House, and the other from Manor House to Netherton Road; a cross-passage was built at Manor House to link the two tunnels and to allow accurate surveys to be transferred between them. The cross-passage was later incorporated into an access tunnel leading from a shaft sunk at the site of Manor House

Section of Victoria Line tunnel lined with unbolted cast-iron segments. Some boltholes are cast into the flange to provide a fixing for cable brackets and equipment.

LTB *official photograph*

substation. The tunnelling was completed in July 1961 and illustrated that a tunnelling speed of 60 feet (18m) a day could be achieved in favourable conditions, which was substantially faster than older methods of construction.

The future southbound experimental tunnel was then extended from the cross passage at the Finsbury Park shaft to make an end-on junction with the southbound Northern City Line just north of Finsbury Park station. Track was then laid along about 1600 feet (490m) of the new tunnel and was connected to the Northern City Line, which allowed the latter's pre-1938 stock trains to be used for vibration, ventilation and other tests in the experimental tunnels. The trackwork in the new tunnel was available for test purposes from Sunday 13th May 1962.

At last, on 20th August 1962, the government announced that the new tube could proceed. The breakthrough is sometimes attributed to a government-commissioned report by two Oxford academics, C. D. Foster and M. E. Beesley, which took factors other than simple finance into account; in other words a cost-benefit analysis. This demonstrated that the social benefits of the Victoria Line would more than justify spending the money re-

Section of Victoria Line tunnel lined with unbolted pre-cast concrete segments showing the fixing holes for cables and equipment, also pre-formed. The shelf in the lower portion of tunnel is designed to reduce the amount of noise above the floor level of the trains.

LTB official photograph *

quired. The cost was now some £56 million to be financed by advances of the government loan. The interest charges were inevitably to be set against higher fares, an arrangement which evoked some criticism in the press, much comparison being drawn with the systems in other major cities where governments at least paid for the running tunnels.

Other factors weighing in favour of the timing include the possibility of showing a political commitment to the new London Transport Board; although this did not take charge until 1st January 1963 it was set up as a result of the 1962 Transport Act which received the Royal Assent on 1st August 1962, only nineteen days prior to Victoria Line authorization. The unemployment situation was also unfavourable to the government of the day and there was a suggestion that constructing the Victoria Line could create a useful number of new jobs.

Later studies into the delays before authorization conclude that the London Transport Executive did everything reasonably possible to persuade the authorities that an early start was needed urgently. However the Executive had always to work through the BTC where it is possible that the sense of urgency was somewhat diluted; a

21

possible result of perceiving a risk that the Victoria Line might be authorized at the expense of the British Railways' modernization programme, which was of more direct interest. This may especially have been so while London Transport's image was a very good one while that of British Railways was rather decrepit.

London Transport's Chairman, Alec Valentine, suggested in 1965 that useful movement in the direction of building (rather than discussing) the line only happened when LT began direct negotiations with the Ministry of Transport during 1961, when the Transport Bill was being prepared. He felt that the Ministry thereby gained a more intimate grasp of the needs and problems of London Transport, and the Victoria Line was an early result.

The Ministry's view was not wholly in accord with that of Valentine. It preferred to suggest that the Victoria Line case was a marginal one in financial terms and that in the battle for capital investment it found difficulty in getting sufficiently near the top of the list. It was finally approved for other reasons, said the Permanent Secretary, though he did not cite political expediency as one of them! But there was common ground between Valentine and the Ministry in observing that the Victoria Line fared quite well in London Transport terms, but not in terms of the Commission as a whole; so whatever other factors were at play, the demise of the BTC is one of undoubted significance.

There remains at the moment plenty of room for discussion about the exact timing of the government go-ahead, nearly 25 years after J. P. Thomas originally perceived the need and usefulness of new tubes in central London. For example, another factor had been the comparatively recent introduction of rolling programmes of capital investment in which Victoria Line expenditure became less unfavourable than it did when specific *ad hoc* annual bids had to be made for the necessary money.

When authority did arrive it caused a dilemma. A feature of the continual hints of 'soon, but not now' was that it was impracticable to keep updating the station designs, with attendant survey and parliamentary costs. Unless considerable further delay was to be caused, the seven-year-old plans for the station fabrics had to be utilized, although recognized no longer to be ideal.

Before describing the construction of the Victoria Line it will be helpful to examine the route which was actually selected and look at some of the difficulties presented and the variations which were made to it.

The preferred tunnel arrangement was one where the stations were built on 'humps' in the track; the gradients tending to slow trains down when approaching platforms, and accelerate them when leaving, resulting in a useful energy saving. Except in a very few instances this was very difficult to do on the Victoria Line where the level rose 130 feet (40m) between Victoria and Finsbury Park, then dropped 100 feet (30m) beneath the Lea Valley before recovering this level again at Wood Street (as the original plan allowed). Furthermore the levels at certain intermediate stations were also fixed by existing conditions, such as the requirements for same-level interchange.

The exact route between Seven Sisters and Walthamstow was only settled shortly before parliamentary approval was sought. Two possible routes had been considered. One envisaged a line mainly in tube tunnel from Seven Sisters which broke surface just short of Wood Street station. The second route saw the line breaking surface just south of Seven Sisters where it would run into a new station combining Seven Sisters and South Tottenham; it would then continue at surface level beside the Tottenham & Forest Gate line to Blackhorse Road, thence in tube, and as the first scheme to Wood Street. Both schemes anticipated intermediate ROUTE C stations at Blackhorse Road and in Walthamstow (Hoe Street). The tube route also allowed Tottenham Hale BR station to be served (reflecting the Working Party's preference) and required a depot site to the north of the line on marshland between Northumberland Park station and Lockwood Reservoir. The surface route envisaged a depot on Walthamstow Marshes, just north of Clapton. Engineering surveys encouraged the planners to favour the tube route.

But changing circumstances warranted further consideration being given to the northern terminus, even in 1961, at a relatively late stage in the line's development. The parliamentary powers allowed for the new railway to surface at Wood Street station to provide cross-platform interchange with Chingford services, with sidings beyond the station for Victoria Line trains to reverse and stable. However, the Chingford line electrification had been completed by November 1960, on the overhead line system, and it is widely stated that the disruption caused by the arrival of the Victoria Line would have been unacceptable. It might be borne in mind that the electrification had not got off to a good start and had been plagued by rolling stock problems which prevented the full service being introduced. Traffic had also increased on the Chingford line and it was decided to review the revised traffic needs and costs of sending the Victoria Line to Wood Street. As a result, it had been decided by the end of the year to abandon the section from Hoe Street to Wood Street. It might perhaps be added that truncating the line, together with a cheaper tunnelling estimate resulting from the experimental work, cut out £4 million of the £5 million increase in costs between 1958 and 1961, and was a factor in the line being given the go-ahead at all.

The initially authorized site for Hoe Street station was at the junction of Hoe Street, High Street and Church Hill. With the loss of the Wood Street portion it was possible to re-align Hoe Street platforms so that they would run under the Eastern Region station instead; interchange with the Chingford line was thus maintained. Authority for the changes was granted in the British Transport Commission Act 1963. The result was a Victoria Line station reached by steps linking the main line platforms to an intermediate concourse, whence escalators led to the tube platforms. Tickets were to be issued and collected by BR staff. Outside the railway station a new bus station was constructed.

The next station was to be at Blackhorse Road, across the road from the existing BR station. It was planned to be a simple two-platform station with the escalators from the street level ticket hall coming down between the platforms. The line then veered almost north-west in order to reach Tottenham Hale. This station would be similar to Blackhorse Road but the ticket hall also served the Eastern Region Cambridge line platforms.

Seven Sisters station was to have three platforms, one of which was primarily intended to serve trains terminating there. Although it had long been the intention to terminate a proportion of the service at Seven Sisters, it was now proposed that the access tracks to and from the depot join the sidings north of the station, re-placing the authorized proposal for this connection to be made north of Tottenham Hale (the change was allowed in the British Transport Commission Act 1957). The station was to have esca-lators at each end of the platforms, one set leading to the BR station in the High Road, where a new joint ticket hall would be built, and the other leading to a concourse beneath the junction of the High Road and Seven Sisters Road. The depot site was near BR's Northumberland Park station on the Cambridge line, and the land taken was effectively waste marshland which required exten-sive draining. A mile-long twin tube connection took the line to the surface where siding and repair facilities were to be available for the whole line.

South of Seven Sisters the line would continue in twin tubes beneath the Seven Sisters Road towards Finsbury Park where the existing Northern City Line low-level platforms were to be taken over. It must be recalled that the 1949 London Plan Working Party's report assumed completion of the partly-constructed pre-war works connecting the Northern City at Drayton Park with new high-level platforms at Finsbury Park (alongside the main line station), and with electrification of the Northern Heights branch to Highgate and Alexandra Palace, for through tube trains from Moorgate and Highbury & Islington.

Although that scheme envisaged part of the Northern City service still terminating in the low-level platforms at Finsbury Park, it was felt there would be little problem in diverting the whole service to the upper platforms, releasing the tube station for Victoria Line trains.

Matters were more complicated by the time detailed engineering plans were drawn up for the Victoria Line. The Northern City extensions had been abandoned and its trains all used the low-level station. While there were now proposals to electrify the BR suburban services through Finsbury Park high-level, with local trains routed onto the main-line size Northern City (so vacating its low-level platforms), no-one knew when this might happen. If the Victoria Line were to be authorized before BR electrification, interim arrangements would be needed for the Northern City Line.

One option was to finish the pre-war link to Finsbury Park high-level, including the new platforms whose steelwork had already been erected (and, as late as 1962, retained at LT's request). This work might have a short life if the electrification later went ahead. Either way, the value of good interchange with the Victoria Line (to give a route to the City) was paramount, and cross-platform interchange at Highbury & Islington would be vital. Another option was simply to curtail the Northern City at Drayton Park diverting passengers to other routes (including an interchange with the Victoria Line at Highbury & Islington).

Regardless of any interim arrangements, it was decided in principle that the Northern City low-level platforms at Finsbury Park had to be taken over. By re-arranging the approach tracks it would be possible to permit same-level interchange between the like directions of flow of the Piccadilly and Victoria Lines, whereas the existing Piccadilly and Northern City platforms were parallel but independent of each other. The southbound Piccadilly Line was diverted through the former northbound Northern City Line platform and the Victoria Line then used the former southbound Northern City and the vacated southbound Piccadilly Line station tunnels.

Between Finsbury Park and King's Cross the Working Party report had not envisaged a station, although one at Barnsbury had been mooted earlier. It was decided by 1951 to shift the route eastwards, via Highbury & Islington, to provide attractive, same-level interchange with the Northern City Line for passengers from the Victoria Line suburbs going to the City, and for West End passengers from Alexandra Palace (1951) or the electrified main line services (1955) – in the event it was the 'Great Northern Electrics' of 1976.

Same-level interchange required construction of two additional platforms. The northbound Northern City Line was re-routed through one of them and was engineered for main-line gauge trains in anticipation of the Eastern Region electrification scheme. The other one, together with the vacated Northern City platform, were destined for the Victoria Line. All four platforms would be linked by escalators with a new surface building over the BR North London Line, giving a new interchange facility with that line. The existing BR ticket hall, Northern City street-level station and lifts would be closed.

At King's Cross the complexity of existing railway tunnels permitted only one site for the Victoria Line platforms. The new line had to thread its way above the Piccadilly Line but just below the tunnels carrying the British Railways services to Moorgate via the Metropolitan 'Widened Lines'. There was to be a reversing siding just north of the station which would otherwise be of the usual twin platform arrangement with escalators leading up to the existing Northern and Piccadilly Line ticket hall, which would be enlarged; a low-level stairway also linked the Victoria Line with these tube lines.

At Euston same-level interchange was sought with the Northern Line (City branch), whose existing tracks shared a single large-bore station tunnel and flanked a narrow island platform with an access at one end leading to the three ageing lifts and the Northern Line (Charing Cross branch) platforms. The arrival of the Victoria Line meant that the existing station tunnel would remain to serve just southbound Northern Line trains while the northbound service would be diverted through a 2500ft (760m) diversion tunnel serving a new northbound platform. The Victoria Line would thread its way between the two Northern Line platforms to provide the same-level interchange. Both the Victoria and Northern Lines ran east–west at Euston, so an odd result of providing same-level, same direction interchange was that southbound trains faced the opposite way on each line, (and likewise northbound). Such interchange also required the Victoria Line to adopt 'right-hand running' through Euston, but practical considerations dictated that the tunnels 'rolled over' each other north of King's Cross, and back again south of Warren Street, so 'wrong direction' running prevailed at these stations too.

Engineering at Euston was further complicated because prior to Victoria Line authorization the BTC was planning wholesale reconstruction of the main line station above. The three aged lifts might not survive the considerable strain upon them if they had to last until the new station facilities were quite ready. It was decided to build a new entrance, ticket hall and escalator shaft to the Charing Cross branch platforms to relieve pressure on the existing lifts and

GT NORTHERN & CITY (ELECTRIC) RAILWAY.
Finsbury Park Station.

Three views of what is now the southbound Victoria Line platform at Finsbury Park.

(Top) In early Great Northern & City Railway days with 'main line' size electric train (looking north).
M.A.C.Horne collection

(Centre) During reconstruction in the mid 1960s (looking north).
LTB *official photograph* *

(Bottom) In 1988 with a Victoria Line train departing (looking south).
R.J.Greenaway

ticket hall. The new facilities would be built to allow incorporation into the planned Victoria Line works – if and when they were authorized. Work began on a temporary entrance and a pair of escalators towards the end of 1961; these came into use on 8th March 1965. Initially the new entrance was only used between 6am and 8pm and the older entrance remained open throughout the day, though now with only two lifts available. The Victoria Line go-ahead in August 1962 meant the eventual installation of a further six escalators and closure of the old ticket hall and lifts.

A change was made on the Euston to Oxford Circus section in diverting the Victoria Line via Warren Street station; this was done on the grounds that it broke an otherwise lengthy section of line in central London and improved public transport access to an increasingly important area. Warren Street was to comprise a simple pair of platforms with escalators leading up to an existing intermediate level between two flights of Northern Line escalators. To increase capacity a third escalator was to replace the fixed stairway in the upper Northern Line flight, now to serve both lines. The ticket hall area was re-arranged but little other alteration was made to the station.

Oxford Circus required comprehensive redevelopment. Throughout the 1950s the station was unable to cope satisfactorily with its existing peak hour traffic and it was inconceivable to contemplate any additional load without wholesale reconstruction. A new ticket hall beneath the 'circus' itself and several new banks of escalators were therefore planned, together with major new low-level subways. Same-level interchange with the Bakerloo Line was a paramount requirement; fortunately the existing Bakerloo platforms were 'outside' the tracks, and this made the design of the interchange with the Victoria Line more straightforward.

Green Park would have a simple two-platform arrangement with escalators leading up to the existing (though much enlarged) ticket hall. At low level a subway connection would link the Victoria and Piccadilly Lines.

Victoria station presented a different problem for the planners. We have already seen that the 1949 plan contemplated the new line continuing southwards towards Croydon; this was still an option being advocated under the ROUTE C banner in 1951. But another London Plan tube (ROUTE D, a south-west to north-east line) was also being actively considered. Because the full extent of both schemes would not be authorized in the short term, an expedient was suggested for ROUTE C to be built north of Victoria and ROUTE D south-west from Victoria, towards Chelsea, Fulham and Wimbledon: the two to be temporarily worked as a single railway. At some later stage the rest of ROUTE D would be built, and ROUTE C could then continue to Croydon. The station design had therefore to allow its temporary use as a terminus, and yet enable the line to be extended both south or south-west, with provision for later adaptation for same-level interchange between the two tube lines.

By the time of the 1955 Act the likelihood of ROUTE D ever being built had further receded, but early extension of ROUTE C towards Wimbledon was still preferred – it was cheaper to build than a southwards extension – and this was reflected in the powers sought. A new ticket hall would be built beneath the main line station forecourt with escalators to the new tube-level island platform, and a separate interchange route would be built to connect with the District Line.

The construction of an underground railway is inevitably a slow and complex affair. Building the Victoria Line from Victoria to Walthamstow took over six years, in spite of efforts to reduce the construction time. The phasing of the complex work at Oxford Circus was the limiting factor in central London; indeed the reconstruction of this station was not only the last major work to be completed, but it was also the first contract to start following the government go-ahead, with exploratory work beneath the 'circus' itself beginning on 20th September, to establish the exact position of the pipes and mains of the utility services. This had to be known before they could be diverted and work begun on the new underground ticket hall. Other difficult parts of the programme included the station works at Victoria, Green Park, Euston and Highbury, the running tunnels between Victoria and Oxford Circus and between Tottenham and Walthamstow, and also the Northern City Line diversion tunnel at Highbury. All these works could be pressed ahead quickly as the engineers had had years to finalise many design and construction details.

By the end of 1963 contracts had been placed for over £22 million worth of work, including all the shields and tunnel lining. Over 20 working shafts had been sunk and over 30 working sites occupied. At Highbury the diversion tunnel for the northbound Northern City Line was under construction while work had begun outside King's Cross main line station in demolishing property to form a working site. At Euston part of the new ticket hall and escalators to the Northern Line (Charing Cross branch) platforms were nearly complete. A massive steel bridge had been erected across Oxford Circus to allow work to begin there on the new ticket hall. Work had started at Victoria on the District Line interchange passages and the associated lengthening eastwards of the District platforms.

By the autumn of 1964 work was proceeding on all the contracts except those for the three northernmost stations, and the value of the work had reached £25 million. By the end of that year 33 shafts had been sunk and 40 working sites were occupied. Running tunnels were being driven from 15 tunnel faces, eight of these using mechanical excavating shields and seven using shields employing hand mining. There were also seven station tunnel shields in use.

Major progress was made during 1965 in pushing ahead the tunnels, with about three-quarters of the running tunnels and over half the station tunnels complete by the year's end. On one tunnelling drive the then world record for soft ground tunnelling was broken with a rate of 470 feet (140m) per week. Ticket halls were complete or well advanced at Seven Sisters, King's Cross, Euston (partly opened in March), Oxford Circus, Green Park and Victoria. Good progress had been made on the escalator shafts and low-level passages at Seven Sisters, Euston, Warren Street, Oxford Circus, Green Park and Victoria. The last three major contracts had been let – for Walthamstow, Blackhorse Road and Tottenham Hale. Extensive work had been undertaken at the Northumberland Park depot site where a temporary track fabrication depot had been built; some tracklaying had begun here and was proceeding into the tunnels towards Seven Sisters station.

1966 saw the completion of all running tunnels (on 20th September) and 23 of the 24 station tunnels. The experimental tunnels north of Finsbury Park were by now integral with the rest of the running tunnels. Although extensive use had been made of the new concrete or flexible iron linings, much of the line had nevertheless utilized traditional bolted iron segments, for example in stations and passageways and where the ground was likely to be unsound (where some use was also made of compressed-air working). In the same year escalator shafts were complete at all but three stations and contracts were placed for substations, cablework and the control room at Euston. Tracklaying proceeded.

The major construction work was substantially wrapped up during 1967. All tunnelling except for a short subway at Oxford Circus was complete and long-welded rails had been laid throughout, having been brought in by special train from Northumberland Park depot to replace temporary track (some of which had been brought down the working shafts rather than by train). When they were no longer needed for access the working shafts were either filled in or utilized for fan or draught relief purposes. Teams were engaged in fitting out the line and stations. The Euston control room shell was completed and equipping began. Northumberland Park depot substation was commissioned and five of the other eight substations were equipped. The finishing work continued during

1968 when the Victoria Line approached its opening, which was to take place in three stages.

The construction of the line had been very intricate, owing to the warren of existing tunnels and passages through which it had to thread its way, and because of the construction and diversion work required at stations in daily use and around tunnels through which trains still ran. The construction programme had been carefully planned by using a system of Network Analysis aided by computer – a fairly revolutionary approach at the time. Although many attempts were made to arrest programme slippages a year was cumulatively lost. Major factors were the time taken to assemble the necessary expertise at the start, and the constant shortage of manpower, especially miners; a boom in the construction industry from 1962 made competition fierce. Ground conditions were sometimes worse than feared, at Oxford Circus nine months were lost in diversions of services, and six months were lost in tunnelling at Euston. The decision to introduce more advanced technology (such as automatic trains) also created delays, especially when deliveries were late anyway. A serious fire at Tottenham Hale introduced further delay and the four stations at the north end of the line were incomplete at the time of opening.

Interestingly, the Kinnear Moodie 'drum digger' tunnelling machine which had fared so well on the experimental tunnels proved to be slightly less superior to the alternative digging machine, of the centre shaft type, made by McAlpine. A Mark II drum digger was devised but was defeated by bad ground before it could fully demonstrate its capabilities. Some of the engineering

One of the tunnel digging machines built by McAlpine. This type has the rotating cutting face attached to a central drive-shaft.
Institution of Civil Engineers

A large new junction tunnel under construction for the westbound Piccadilly Line diversion at Finsbury Park. Piccadilly Line trains continued to run in the carefully supported existing tunnel in the foreground until it could be dismantled. *LTB official photograph* *

involved was quite remarkable and a description of some of the larger works follows.

Diversion of existing railway tunnels was required at Euston (described already) and at Highbury and Finsbury Park. Apart from driving new lengths of tunnel, the work involved the construction of junction tunnels around the existing lines, with excavation of the surrounding ground, reached by new headings or shafts. As this work proceeded the large-diameter junction tunnel was gradually formed and new tunnel segments erected, the existing tunnel being carefully supported within the new tunnel while this was done. Then the old tunnel-iron was dismantled and the track was temporarily supported until a more permanent trackbed could be laid. Finally, track was installed in the new tunnels and the line diverted.

At Finsbury Park, the absence of BR electrification and the need to economise on capital expenditure meant that the preferred option to release the tube platforms was to cut back the Northern City Line to Drayton Park, which took effect after the last train on 3rd October 1964. A coach service shuttle ran between the two stations until the Victoria Line opened; the traffic day was also shortened to operate from about 6:45am to 8pm (which times prevailed until closure in 1975 prior to transfer to British Rail).

Work then began on the 3150ft (960m) diversion of the south-bound Piccadilly Line through the former Northern City north-bound platform. Once constructed, the route was switched at the northern end simply by commissioning new signalling and chang-ing the (temporary) points. However there was a 5ft (1·5m) differ-ence in level where the old and new routes entered the southern junction tunnel, about 200ft (60m) north of Arsenal station. This required the old line to be supported on a massive trestle. On the day of the change-over the trestle had to be demolished and removed, and the track laid in on the new alignment to connect with that already laid in the diversion tunnel – an intensive task completed by 2pm on Sunday 3rd October 1965, having started at close of traffic on Saturday night.

At Highbury & Islington the northbound Northern City Line was switched through a new platform. To speed up the work on the 2450ft (750m) diversion, the Northern City train service was re-arranged after 8pm each night from 11th May 1963 (until mid-evening services were withdrawn in 1964), freeing the northbound tunnel in the Highbury area for the engineers. A single-line shuttle service ran on the southbound line between Finsbury Park and Essex Road, where it connected with another shuttle, on the northbound line, between there and Moorgate. For a brief period tunnel possession was required in the Finsbury Park area when the northern shuttle operated on the northbound line from Finsbury Park to Drayton Park, thence the southbound line as far as Essex Road. The Highbury diversion tunnel and new platform came into use on Sunday 15th August 1965. Work then began to plug the new southbound Victoria Line into the vacant tunnel and to mod-ernize the old platform.

Oxford Circus was the biggest station reconstruction. Essen-tially, a new ticket hall was constructed beneath the 'circus' with escalators down to an intermediate level and further escalators down to lower concourses. These were built between pairs of Victoria and Bakerloo Line platforms, with which the Victoria Line offered same-level interchange. An escalator also led from the intermediate level to the Central Line. The new construction was to be used mainly for 'Way In' traffic, leaving the existing three Bakerloo and two Central escalators and ticket hall areas available for the 'Way Out' traffic. In addition, a major re-arrangement of low-level passageways was required to ease flows and to replace some passages which would be cut through by the new running tunnels. The old subways were replaced in a carefully phased programme, the station having to remain fully operational throughout. Some of the construction took place in waterlogged ground and chemical consolidation was needed.

It had been decided to bridge the entire road surface of the 'circus' with a massive steel deck, popularly known as the Oxford Circus Umbrella, to facilitate the construction of the new ticket hall. The 600 tons (610t) of prefabricated steel sections were erected during the August Bank Holiday weekend of 1963, the Circus and some surrounding streets being closed from early afternoon on Saturday 3rd August until 6:30am on Tuesday 6th August. This decking initially had an area of 2500 square yards (2090 sq m), including the ramps which took the traffic up to deck level, 3ft 6ins (1·07m) above the road surface. The deck sections were mounted on a steel framework which itself sat on some 25 concrete cylinders, which had been sunk through the road surface previously. The temporary arrangements allowed traffic to flow westbound along Oxford Street and southbound along Regent Street, the return flows using other roads.

The Umbrella was extended about 100ft (30m) eastwards along Oxford Street during the 1966 August Bank Holiday to allow construction of the subway linking the existing ticket hall to the new one, the working period being similar to that of 1963. Its task complete, the Umbrella was removed during the Easter holiday weekend of 1968, the area being closed off from 11:30pm on Thursday 11th April until the very early morning on Tuesday 16th April.

During the time the deckwork was in position the new ticket hall area and upper escalators were excavated and public utility services re-routed, many of the materials required being delivered to the working site at night through holes created by removing decking panels. In due course the new ticket hall roof, which was to support the roadway above, was completed and the load of the Umbrella bridge was gradually transferred from the special columns to the permanent roadway.

Another difficult part of the work at Oxford Circus arose from the construction of the southbound Victoria Line station tunnel. The new tunnel was required to pass just beneath the third basement level of the Peter Robinson department store and it was necessary to spread some of the load of the building before tunnelling began. From the working shaft at Cavendish Square a 250yds (230m) access tunnel was driven to a point beneath the store. A pre-stressed concrete raft was then constructed below the basement to spread the load. The lower side of the raft was formed of weak concrete and intersected the line of the future southbound tunnel roof. The crown of the station tunnel was eventually driven through the bottom of the raft, and as each of the specially reinforced tunnel rings was completed it assumed some of the load of the building.

At Victoria, the main line station had been built on the back-filled site of the former Grosvenor Canal basin, which was originally a reservoir for the Chelsea Waterworks Company and then adapted to take water-borne freight. Chemical treatment was needed to consolidate both this ground and adjacent water-bearing sand and gravel before the Victoria Line tunnels could be constructed. During sewer diversion work part of the former canal basin walls were encountered.

Just north of Victoria station the running tunnels passed beneath the site of the former Watney brewery which had deep foundation piles. To speed up the work on the northbound tunnel drive, the drum digger was fitted with hardened cutting teeth which allowed it to chew its way slowly through the concrete piles as they were encountered, though this did put a strain on the equipment.

Detailed plans for equipping the tube tunnels and stations had begun in the 1950s. During the early years the Victoria Line was not intended to differ in any material way from other Underground lines, other than by having all the latest trains and equipment. By the time of authorization, however, widespread automation was favoured, to reduce the need for large numbers of additional staff who were becoming difficult to recruit and were absorbing an increasing share of the traffic receipts. Four new developments were adopted for the Victoria Line: automatic ticket issuing and checking; stations run from a single 'operations room'; automatic routeing of trains supervised from a central control room; and automatically driven trains.

London Transport had sold a large volume of tickets from automatic ticket machines for many years, and for the Victoria Line it was desired both to increase this proportion further and to devise a method of checking the tickets automatically in electronic barriers, rather than by traditional manual checks. In doing this, LT worked closely with the Advanced Data Corporation, an American company which was developing similar equipment. Initial experiments took place in 1963 with a selection of different types of encoding possibilities, some of which were tried on tickets to see how they withstood handling. The following year an experimental barrier entered service for 'Way In' passengers at Stamford Brook station, which used specially printed tickets. Further barriers were tried subsequently at Ravenscourt Park, Chiswick Park and Acton Town, using a variety of special tickets and encoding techniques. As a result of these experiments a workable design of barrier evolved, using a system of card tickets backed with an iron oxide coating which could be encoded magnetically. The new tickets were coloured yellow to distinguish them from the then existing range, which could only be checked manually.

To test the concept realistically it was decided to have a full scale trial at Hammersmith (District & Piccadilly) station in 1966. A new ticket office was constructed centrally in the main ticket hall and 14 free-standing automatic ticket machines were also provided. All could issue the new tickets and the ticket office could also issue encoded season tickets. On one wall of the ticket office a large self-service 'Multi-fare' machine issued several types of ticket to any Underground station; there was also a note-changing machine designed to handle ten-shilling (50p) and one-pound notes. A feature of these two machines was that the booking clerks could service them from within the office. Six automatic gates were provided, three for 'Way In' traffic, and three for 'Way Out', for passengers holding yellow tickets. The manned barriers were retained because of the unencoded tickets issued by other stations. The ticket collector no longer dealt with excess fares owed by passengers, who were directed to a separate ticket office window within the barrier line, which issued encoded excess fare tickets for use in the automatic gates.

The experiment was deemed very successful and it was decided to introduce automatic ticket issuing and checking on the Victoria Line as a prelude to systemwide introduction. Since this authority was received only in May 1967, after much of the ticket hall construction had already been completed, some delay was inevitable as alterations were made to ticket hall areas to accommodate the new equipment and revised passenger flows, but the changes were all achieved within the existing box structures. Not all the installations were complete even when the line had reached Victoria, and initially a greater reliance was placed on traditional manual ticket inspection than had been planned.

The operations room philosophy presumed that the station supervisor might be used to greater effect if he resided in purpose-built accommodation with efficient communication facilities; these would include closed-circuit television monitoring of the rest of the station, direct line telephone links to all key points and public address facilities to all areas of the station.

A full scale experiment was therefore conducted at Holborn station, starting in December 1962. The operations room was constructed high above the concourse at the bottom of the four main escalators. The station supervisor viewed the busy scene below through 'one-way' mirrored windows. Each of the four main platforms was equipped with at least one television camera monitored from the operations room, which was also given controls to turn, tilt and focus most of the cameras. Full public address facilities were given, and a new feature was the introduction of 'Passenger Information Points' on the platforms – an intercom system allowing passengers wanting information to speak to the supervisor (Russell Square platforms were later added to the system). Also considered successful, operations rooms were incorporated into the Victoria Line planning process.

The signalling system on the Underground had been largely automatic since just after the turn of the century, except, of course, at junctions and reversing points where signal cabins remained necessary. But even here the tendency had been to build new signal cabins to cover increasingly larger areas, often at the cost of closing several smaller cabins. In the late 1950s experiments had taken place on the Northern Line to automate some of the cabins in the central area by replacing the signalmen with programme machines. These machines incorporated a long plastic strip containing punched holes which represented train movements through the relevant junctions. As each train passed through the junction the strip, mounted between rollers, moved along (or stepped) to the next row of holes. The coded commands produced by the machines were then used to operate the levers on the signal frame itself.

To supervise the action of these machines a small control room was built at Leicester Square incorporating an illuminated track diagram of the central area of the Northern Line, together with push button controls to adjust the working of the programme machines in the event of trains running out of sequence, or to operate the points and signals by remote control. It was agreed to install a similar system on the entire Victoria Line, supervised from a purpose-built control room at Euston.

Automatically driven trains had long been a quest of railway operators, in particular as a way of preventing trains overrunning signals at danger. Automation also suggested that the crew could be reduced from two to one per train, an attractive goal on a new railway, especially at a difficult time for recruitment. London Transport's particular desire for automatic operation was boosted by the peculiar circumstances of deep-level tube operation in single-track tunnels: in the unusual event of the train driver becoming incapacitated it was expected that the guard (who was trained to drive) would get the train to the next station. If, however, there was no guard then some other means of extricating the train quickly had to be devised – automation appeared to meet this need.

After initial experimentation some of the proposed equipment was installed on track between South Ealing and Acton Town which, during the day, was reserved for the operation of test trains; a District Line car was fitted with the trial train-borne equipment. The results were promising, so the next stage was to transfer the trackside equipment to a stretch of line between Stamford Brook and Ravenscourt Park. A District Line driving car was fitted with prototype train-borne equipment and trials began in passenger service in April 1963. The special car was coupled to the east end of a District Line passenger train which operated normally for the majority of the time. However, when the train arrived at Stamford Brook (eastbound) the driver selected automatic operation and the train proceeded all the way to Ravenscourt Park without the need for the driver to touch anything, stopping and starting at any intermediate red signals as required. This experiment, too, was deemed very successful.

Following the results of this small-scale experiment it was then decided to engage in a much larger trial. The Central Line branch between Woodford and Hainault was (and still is) mainly operated as an independent shuttle service. The Central Line was also blessed with three experimental 8-car trains (classed as 1960 stock) which were non-standard with the fleet then in course of delivery. The whole of the Woodford–Hainault section of line was equipped with facilities for automatic train operation, and the prototype trains converted into five 4-car automatic trains. Equipping was completed during April 1964, and the automatic trains were then tested.

The prototype equipment used on the Hainault shuttle service did suggest a number of relatively minor improvements, but on the whole it performed most satisfactorily and the decision was made to equip the Victoria Line for the operation of fully automatic trains. As installed, the Victoria Line signalling system therefore differed radically from that used elsewhere in the British Isles. Automatic operation relied on sequences of auto-drive commands being transmitted from 'spots' on the track, with the running of the train at all times being governed by one of three safety codes which had to be continuously received by the train; both the commands and safety codes were received by pick-up coils mounted on the train's leading bogie. With most of the 'signals' effectively replaced by electronic codes only a very few conventional signals were installed, mainly for use by ballast trains and in emergency manual working.

There were many thoughts about the train design. In the early 1950s it was proposed to use a new train (the 1952 stock) then on the drawing board. As the years rolled by the proposed design emulated the latest design on other lines. Towards the end of the decade some thought went into the use of articulated trains, where bogies were shared between adjacent cars. The advantage was that this increased the flexibility in locating the doors, to help reduce train boarding times. Trains of all-motored, regeneratively braked, fairly short cars were contemplated, with 10-car trains (of two 5-car units). However the design relied on the very shallow curves on the

One of the Central Line's 1960 stock prototype units after conversion to automatic oper-
tion on the Woodford–Hainault shuttle service. It may be seen that the cab-side doors
ave been sealed and the tripcock reset cord piped up to the cab door to avoid the need for
he train operator to leave the cab. *LTB official photograph* *

Victoria Line and it would have been difficult to get the trains to
Acton Works for overhaul over Piccadilly Line tracks. When the
Victoria Line nominal tunnel size was finally set at 12ft (3·7m) it
became hard to devise an articulated carbody structure giving a
sufficient distance between bogie centres to give a satisfactory train
layout and it was simpler to retain the traditional 8-car train
formation.

The main starting point was therefore the 1960 prototype stock
which already indicated the direction of the prevailing thinking.
The 1960 stock adopted several new features, chief among which
were a new body profile and much larger, double glazed windows.
Each 4-car unit was intended to comprise two motor cars (with
driving cabs) and a pair of intermediate trailers. Each motor car was
fitted with four traction motors (instead of two as hitherto) with
pairs of motors connected in permanent series, another new feature. These principles formed the foundation of the Victoria Line
trains.

By late 1963 or early 1964 the design was based on the 1960
stock underframe but with a restyled body incorporating a number
of new features and which could accommodate automatic operation. Models and mock-ups were built and studied, and these
appear to have been heavily influenced by the design consultants.
Within the next year several fundamental changes had been made,
including a re-profiled body (but retaining the wrap-round cab
windows) and less 'angular' interior fittings.

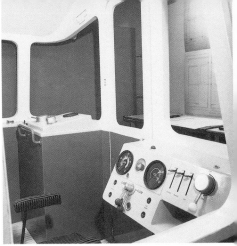

(Left) A mock-up of the car interior of the new Victoria Line stock in 1964 and *(Right)* a mock-up of the proposed interior of a Victoria Line train in 1964; a somewhat radical layout which was not adopted.   LTB *official photographs*

The 30½ trains which emerged were of 8-cars, divided into two identical 4-car units. The cars at the ends of each unit were equipped with driving cabs and each axle was fitted with its own traction motor: the intermediate two cars were trailers. The driving cabs were (for safety reasons in view of automatic working) not equipped with side cab doors but instead had a sliding droplight window for the operator to look through, the window being locked and proved closed before the train could start. The cab controls were laid out primarily with automatic operation in mind, but a

A 1964 scale model of the proposed new Victoria Line trains. To allow staff access to the cab (not equipped with side doors) 'catwalk' platforms and handrails were considered on the cab front (an idea later used on the 1972 Mk II stock).   LTB *official photograph*

combined driving and braking controller was provided for emergency and shunting use. Two buttons were provided in order to start the train, and these were duplicated on each side of the cab. The trains were not designed to be uncoupled under service conditions, which was once the practice on the Underground but had largely ceased in the previous decade (in 1959 it had been the intention to run 30 8-car trains per hour in the peaks and 20 4-car trains per hour off-peak). Another new feature to be included in the design was a public address system, although this had also been tested on the 1960 stock.

The new trains began to be delivered to LT at its West Ruislip depot from September 1967, and after final equipping and initial testing each of the units was transferred to Hainault depot for trials in passenger service on the Woodford–Hainault shuttle, operating automatically. The first trains were then hauled by battery locomotive from Hainault to Northumberland Park depot via Leyton and British Rail tracks, the temporary rail link between the depot and the adjacent Eastern Region lines (initially used for delivery of materials) being used. The link was later removed, allowing the flood prevention wall around the depot to be completed; this was required because the depot site was below the flood level of the nearby River Lea (and the adjacent Eastern Region lines had been engulfed in a flood in 1947). Later Victoria Line trains were delivered via a link with the Piccadilly Line at Finsbury Park.

During the construction period prices had inevitably risen, and the 1962 estimate of £56·1 million had increased by £6·8 million during the 6½ years taken to build the line. Additional money had also been made available to cover various items not originally allowed for, such as automatic fare collection, automatic trains and other sundry items, which amounted to £3·5 million. A roughly similar amount was also put aside for contingencies.

It had originally been assumed that LT would have to start paying interest out of its revenue not long after construction started – rising to several million pounds a year. In March 1964 the Minister authorized interest to be 'capitalized' (that is, added to the total government advance) at least until 1967. The effect was that interest enough to warrant a fares increase would not be charged during the line's construction when, it was argued, passengers were actually getting a worse service because of the disruption. However it did add £5·3 million to the £70 million cost of the line which would increase interest charges when it did open. A 'modest' increase in fares was therefore forecast. Some wry observations were made that the passengers benefiting most from the line would be those making substantially shorter journeys as a result. The charge-by-distance fares system then in force suggested

A further mock-up of proposed Victoria Line rolling stock in 1965. This is largely the design which was adopted. *LTB official photograph*

A unit of 1967 tube stock at Woodford not long after delivery. One of the pick-up coils for the automatic equipment may be seen in the foreground, just below the end of the car to the left of the tail light. *LTB official photograph*

that these people would therefore pay less than hitherto, while non-Victoria Line users paid more.

It had been the intention, in 1962, to open the Victoria Line in stages, with Stage 1 opening on 1st September 1967, and the remaining two stages opening at three-monthly intervals. The phased opening principle still held good after programme slippage. Among the many reasons, it made sense to start earning revenue as soon as possible, it re-opened a rail link between Finsbury Park and Highbury & Islington, it allowed the relatively lightly used northern section of the line to test the new equipment under operational conditions, and it allowed many of the new staff to train and acclimatize to the new line before it became really busy.

The first section of line to open was therefore the Walthamstow to Highbury section, which began without ceremony at start of traffic on Sunday 1st September 1968, exactly a year behind programme (the timetable had been operated, without passengers, from 26th August). Shortly before opening, Walthamstow Hoe Street station was renamed Walthamstow Central. At first a 4-minute service operated in the rush hours; trains reversed in the southbound platform at Highbury during the morning peak, and

nterior of 1967 stock trailer car, with longitudinal seating throughout to maximise the area available for standing. The motor cars were fitted with transverse seating in the centre bay to allow equipment to be placed beneath. *LTB official photograph* *

(Left) Interior of driving cab of 1967 stock car and *(Right)* close-up of driver's controls showing the twin start buttons and the large 'Vigilance' button, which has to be kept depressed when the train is operating in 'Slow Manual' working without safety codes.　*LTB official photographs* *

the northbound in the evening, to provide the best connections for City workers using the Northern City Line. All trains ran to Walthamstow during the peak hours with a proportion turned back at Seven Sisters during the off-peak. A feature of the three northern stations was the provision of car parks.

On Saturday 7th September there were widespread alterations to bus routes in London as part of the first stage of the much heralded Bus Reshaping Plan. In Walthamstow a system of feeder services was created to operate into the new (but not quite complete) bus station, built to provide good interchange with the new Victoria Line. Another system of feeder buses served Finsbury Park station, and various changes were also made to a number of trunk routes.

The next section of railway, to Warren Street, opened three months later on 1st December, again without ceremony (timetabled running of empty trains began on 25th November). This time trains reversed in the new southbound platform there, and at this stage the northbound platform was not used. The service pattern and intervals remained similar to those prevailing under Stage 1. On reaching Warren Street, the scissors crossover at Highbury was simplified, and became a trailing emergency crossover.

44

The cross-central London link to Oxford Circus, Green Park and Victoria, and the official opening of the new line, came on 7th March 1969 (timetabled trial running began on 24th February). From this point onwards the Victoria Line became a very busy railway. By May/June 1970 the busiest section, between Victoria and Green Park, was carrying 15,000 passengers in one direction during the peak evening hour. This compares well with the 1955 estimate of 14,000. The annual traffic in passenger miles carried on the new line was estimated as 229 million. The initial train service over the section from Victoria to Seven Sisters was 2–2½ minutes during the peak, half the service being projected on to Walthamstow. A further stage of bus reshaping, along the Seven Sisters Road and through the West End, took place on 24th January 1970 after new travelling patterns had settled down; the emphasis was on encouraging passengers to switch to the new tube.

The public found the beginnings of what then was regarded as the most modern urban railway in the world: smart, spacious ticket halls, gleaming escalators with their brushed metallic finishes, platforms tiled in two-tone blue/grey with bright metallic trim and coloured motifs (different at each station) along the platform seat recesses, and smart new automatically driven trains. The styling was heavily influenced by LT's own design panel and the work of their external consultants, Design Research Unit. Many of the new features had previously been shown to the public at an exhibition at The Design Centre, in London, in 1967.

A platform view of a typical Victoria Line central London station. The white melamine roof, light blue-grey and dark grey wall tiling and coloured motifs in the seat recesses are standard features, together with the 'Victoria Line blue' enamelled station name frieze.

LTB official photograph

While all the stations were broadly similar in design there were detail changes. Between Victoria and King's Cross the station name 'bulls-eyes' were on internally illuminated glass panels, while at other stations they were in the usual enamelled form but floodlit. At most stations the ceiling was finished in white melamine sheeting which distributed the fluorescent light evenly over the platforms. North of Seven Sisters a more economical roof finish was applied where the tunnel segments were simply painted black and the illumination installed in a wide white trough to reflect the light downwards.

Power supply for the new line was derived from nine new substations, at Forest Road, Seven Sisters, Manor House, Drayton Park, Cloudesley Road, Cobourg Street, Dover Street, Gillingham Street and at the depot at Northumberland Park. Each was remotely supervised from a control room at Manor House. The high tension supply was obtained from the Underground's main generating station at Lots Road, which was modernized and provided with higher capacity equipment to take on the additional load (the power station at Greenwich was modernized at about the same time, primarily to assist during periods of peak load).

Walthamstow Central, typical of a Victoria Line northern station, similar in most respects to the general finish elsewhere but with unclad roof and troughed lighting.

LTB official photograph *

The signalling control (or 'regulating') room at Euston was available shortly before the first stage of the line opened, and was designed to accommodate both the Victoria Line as built and its southwards extension to Brixton, about which more below. It also had provision for controlling the signalling on the Northern Line, whose controls were transferred from other sites a few years later. The signalling and pointwork at Walthamstow, Seven Sisters, Northumberland Park depot outlet, King's Cross and Victoria were normally under the control of local programme machines which set up the routes required through electro-mechanical 'interlocking machines', which retained the element of mechanical interlocking of signals and points which would otherwise be found in conventional signal boxes. The programme machine control could if necessary be over-ridden either by the train regulator or by the new train-generated destination apparatus (called 'Identra'). Crossovers also existed at Highbury and Warren Street; at these sites the signalling was normally operated automatically for through running, although the regulator could set up other routes as required and automatic train-reversing facilities were also available.

Communications were considered important on the new line and

47

The interior of the central control room at Euston in 1970. The Victoria Line controller is sitting at the left-hand desk while the train regulator is sitting at the lower level in front of the illuminated track diagram of the line. The right-hand desk is occupied by the Northern Line controller.   *LTB official photograph*

a major advance was made with the Carrier-Wave system which put trains in constant touch with the control room, even while moving (on other lines trains then had to stop before contact could be made). As the train operator was now the only member of staff on each train, arrangements were made to allow him to get help easily, in addition to Carrier-Wave. A special 'Calling-On' light was provided at the back of each train which the operator could activate from the front cab; this authorized the following train to move up to the calling train to render assistance. A short-wave inter-train radio was also provided for use under these circumstances. A feature at platform level was the provision on each platform of three emergency plungers, the operation of which interacted with the automatic train driving circuitry to stop any train in the immediate area. Another facility on in-town platforms were the Passenger Information Points to the station operations room, following the Holborn experiment.

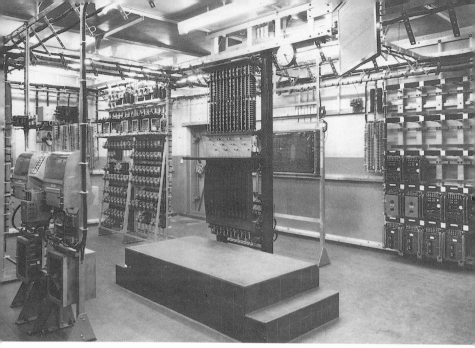

he Interlocking Machine Room at Northumberland Park. On the left are two programme
machines on which all the train movements are stored and which call for routes to be set up
t the correct time. In the centre is the interlocking machine itself; air motors operate the
evers laterally, subject to traditional electrical and mechanical locking. The levers operate
ignals and points as required and in an emergency can be controlled manually.

LTB official photograph *

The depot was provided with three workshop roads and nine
roads with maintenance pits, allowing minor repairs to be performed. Eleven double-length stabling roads were also provided,
all of which were under cover. Because of the distance from the
main Victoria Line the depot was, and still is, unusual in having a
scheduled train service to and from Seven Sisters for staff access,
and a short platform (resited once) is situated in the depot for this
purpose.

Having explained how a working railway was produced from the
point when the Act of Parliament of 1955 crystallized the northern
section, it is now necessary to see what befell the proposed section
south of Victoria. As mentioned earlier the 1955 Act had
authorized an alignment which allowed a choice of extension
south-westwards towards Fulham or south towards Stockwell, the
former possible routeing being preferred. But an LT report of 1958
studied possible routeings carefully, and compared them with
possible extension of the Bakerloo south of Elephant & Castle, for
which powers already existed; the report presumed that extension
of both lines could not be afforded.

The study concluded that a Victoria Line extension to Fulham and Wimbledon would not be very good value for money, nor significantly improve public transport facilities. On the other hand an extension to Croydon would also be poor value because construction would be expensive and traffic south of Streatham would be comparatively light. Extension only as far as Streatham, or, better still, Brixton, would be worthwhile and achieve a useful relief of traffic on the Northern Line. Any Victoria Line extension was felt more valuable than Bakerloo extension to Camberwell, but the report noted that if the BTC felt committed to Camberwell then that line should be extended further (to Brixton) in lieu of the Victoria Line. The report was accepted as the basis of future tube planning for south London, with the Victoria Line extension to Brixton (or Streatham) the preferred option.

An early manifestation of the revised thinking appeared in the British Transport Commission Act 1960, which authorized the sidings beyond the platforms at Victoria to be re-aligned. The station would have two platforms, but the tracks were now to continue in a gradual curve to the south, to lead into four sidings, the outer two of which allowed for conversion into future running lines. At the southern end of the platforms escalators would lead into a new ticket hall beneath the Southern Region station forecourt, while farther back along the platforms additional escalators would lead to a concourse beneath the District Line tracks, from which interchange passages would emerge. Any pretensions to be able to accommodate the now defunct ROUTE D were abandoned.

By 1963 the Victoria Line had been authorized and London Transport was freed of the impoverished British Transport Commission. However, under the 1962 Transport Act both British Railways and London Transport were required to provide properly co-ordinated transport services in London. To fulfil this statutory obligation a joint planning committee was soon established – the Passenger Transport Planning Committee for London. An early decision was made that the Victoria Line ought to be extended at least as far as Brixton, with intermediate stations at Vauxhall and Stockwell. The alignment to Fulham was again considered but the line could not serve Fulham as well as Brixton and the former was officially abandoned – at least for Victoria Line purposes.

The Committee's view was officially expressed in their (unpublished) report of 1965 – 'A Railway Plan for London'. They noted the earlier proposal for a line from Victoria to Croydon, and that this had to be ruled out because of the enormous cost and the expected stagnation of inner-suburban traffic. But they felt that sufficient justification still existed for a limited extension to Brixton only, about 3½ miles (5·6km). Much of the justification rested on the new interchange facilities which would be opened up with the Southern Region and the buses at Brixton and Vauxhall, and the relief of the Northern Line north of Stockwell. If extension beyond Brixton were ever justified they felt that Crystal Palace rather than Croydon would be the objective.

Plans were drawn up, and powers sought in the 1965–66 Parliamentary Session, the Bill receiving Royal Assent on 9th August 1966. In fact, in March 1966 the government had given approval in principle for the scheme, but immediate authority only for preparatory measures, including purchase of tunnel segments. The LT view was that it would be most economical if the tunnelling teams working on the main section of line could be switched to the Brixton extension with the minimum of delay, as it would take some time to re-assemble an experienced team if the existing miners were allowed to disperse. Final Ministerial approval was given on 4th August 1967, and a measure of continuity was achieved. The estimated cost of this extension was £15·9 million.

The significance of the authority to begin was not the relative speed of its arrival (though that was welcome), rather the news that the extension might in due course receive an 'infrastructure grant' (government money given for new works and not loaned), as comparable road schemes had received for years. London (Regional) Transport has continued to receive similar grants from its masters ever since. The grants were initially made under the Transport Act 1968.

The ground south of Victoria was not as amenable to tunnelling as on much of the northern section of line, so rotary tunnelling machines were not used and hand mining with Greathead shields was adopted; the average rate of progress was about 150ft (45m) per week. An unusual hazard existed on the section between Victoria and the River. Several miners reported the existence of a ghost in the southbound tunnel workings, alleged to be near the site where the line passed beneath an old graveyard or plague pit. The 'large black presence' is reported to have induced some consternation at the time.

Vauxhall station site posed major problems. It adjoined the River Thames, close to the outlet of the culverted River Effra, at that point known as Vauxhall Creek; there was therefore much water about, and the clay was overlain by water-bearing gravel. Other complications were the many nearby sewers, and concurrent major road reconstruction, which itself influenced the siting of the ticket hall and access subways. The work was phased, with numerous road diversions made as ticket hall construction progressed. Just below street level the water could be kept out by means of coffer-dams, but the ground through which the escalator shaft was

Stockwell ticket hall showing various features typifying the Victoria Line. On the left wa are the ticket office windows with (beyond the barrier) a window for excess fares. In th middle foreground are the automatic barriers for inwards and outwards traffic, with luggage roller in the middle. In the middle background is the mirrored front of the statio operations room, the mirrors actually disguising one-way glass. On the right hand side a banks of '510' automatic change-giving ticket machines and prominent fares lists t encourage passengers to serve themselves. *LTB official photograph*

to be sunk had initially to be frozen solid (a technique first used at Tottenham Hale).

At Stockwell the new platforms would flank those already existing on the Northern Line. Perhaps ironically the Victoria Line works disturbed the access to the wartime deep shelter tunnels, some passages to which had then to be resited. The ground in the area was partially unsound; one Victoria Line tunnel had to be excavated within six feet (1·8m) of the Northern Line. This was very difficult work and at one point a subsidence caused Northern Line services to be interrupted. The existing Northern Line street level station was replaced with a substantially larger joint station on a similar, but enlarged site. The existing pair of escalators was retained and an additional shaft was sunk containing a third escalator and fixed stairway.

The site of Brixton station lay on the busy Brixton Road in the town centre and was served by numerous bus routes as well as the nearby British Rail station, although (like Vauxhall) no direct BR interchange was provided. A twin platform station with two escalators and a fixed stairway was constructed. Beyond the station were twin overrun and siding tunnels, curving to the south and pointing, perhaps a little optimistically, towards Herne Hill to which point they reach nearly half way. To service the extension an additional nine trains (72 cars) were added to the existing rolling stock order and the total number of cars required rose to 316. The extra trains required an additional 5-road car shed at Northumberland Park depot, together with other minor alterations.

The extension took about four years to build and was ready for opening on 23rd July 1971, after trial running from 12th July. The ceremony was performed by H. R. H. Princess Alexandra during the morning, and the public service began at 3pm the same day. The public soon took to the extension, where they found the station finishes and equipment similar to those on the northern section of the railway.

The only additional controlled signalling site was at Brixton where programme machines were provided. Brixton had a scissors crossover north of the station incorporating power-operated 'switch-diamonds' in the central crossing (an idea first used on the Underground on the Central London Railway in 1912); while these successfully gave a smoother, high speed approach to the station they were a maintenance liability and a normal diamond crossing was substituted in August 1983. The southward extension allowed replacement of the scissors crossover north of Victoria station by a trailing crossover. Power to the extension was fed via additional substations at Stockwell and Brixton.

But this is not quite the end of the story. During the early planning of the Brixton extension the possibility of a station between Victoria and the River was mooted. When powers were sought a route was selected permitting construction of a station in the future if justified. It was not among those authorized in 1967 as the traffic and financial case was at best marginal. However there was strong local support, and the balance was altered when the Crown Estate (a major local landowner) offered easements free for the station site. Although the cost was still not wholly justified financially, government approval arrived on 28th June 1968, and Pimlico – the sixteenth station on the Victoria Line – became a reality. Again an infrastructure grant was made.

Because of its late authorization Pimlico was not ready when the Brixton extension opened, although it was complete at platform level; trains passed through at reduced speed. The opening ceremony was performed by the Lord Mayor of Westminster on 14th September 1972, and the station served passengers from 3pm that afternoon. The total cost of the Brixton extension was about £21·5 million consisting of a 75 per cent grant from the government and the balance from the Greater London Council (GLC), by now LT's masters.

On the subject of ownership it should be noted that for most of

Northumberland Park depot in early 1988. The car sheds are on the left, the lifting shop is behind the lighting mast, and the inspection roads, with pits, are to the right. On the far right may be seen construction work for the additional four-road car shed (commissioned in summer 1988). *M.A.C.Horne*

its life the Victoria Line had been a part of the London Transport Executive, which existed from 1970 and reported to the GLC. From 29th June 1984 the organization passed once more into the hands of central government and was restyled London Regional Transport. Under a provision of the enabling Act a subsidiary company was established on 29th March 1985 called London Underground Limited, and on 1st April 1985 the London Underground system passed into the hands of this new company.

So how has the Victoria Line fared since it opened? It is undoubtedly a very busy line and there is no question that it has proved an extremely valuable addition to the London Underground. Not only is it difficult to imagine how Londoners managed without the line for so long, it is also difficult to imagine how financial doubts could have inhibited a start for so many years. Ironically, after accepting the interest-bearing loan from the government, requiring higher fares, London Transport's transfer from central government to the Greater London Council resulted in the whole capital debt being written off. Years of argument thus failed to achieve any particular object, except delay.

Most of the equipment used on the Victoria Line has stood up well to the heavy punishment it has received over the last twenty years or so. In particular the automatic driving system continues to

54

operate exceptionally well in view of its age and technical obsolescence (remembering that transistorized equipment was relatively new in the early 1960s!). Other features did not prove as successful in real life as had been hoped, thus the Passenger Information Points are now redundant and the inter-train short-wave emergency radio has been removed. The station tiling has also been a perennial minor problem in that much of it has become loose and the tiles are inclined to fall off and leave unsightly patches, a problem even today. It is also slightly difficult to recall that the line is now getting old and equipment is having to be renewed. The auto-drive boxes have recently been replaced by a more modern type with a built-in memory system, and it is intended shortly to replace the ageing Carrier-Wave equipment with modern train radios to link the operators to the control room.

The automatic fare collection system faded away gradually. It was not pursued systemwide for several reasons, not the least of which was cost. The huge number of unencoded tickets presented at Victoria Line stations, which were issued on other lines or by British Rail, meant that no staff savings could be made; the exit gates thus became a liability and were removed in 1972. Entry gates were retained as these did encourage passengers to buy tickets, although the coding was greatly simplified and encoded season tickets were withdrawn. In recent years a new systemwide ticket system has been developed requiring the use of entirely new equipment and new self-contained ticket office suites which will supersede all the original Victoria Line ticket offices. All the old-style automatic ticket barriers have now been removed from Victoria Line stations but at those in the central area more modern automatic entry and exit barriers are in the process of installation, which should permit the removal of manned barriers altogether.

The same-level interchange at Highbury came to full fruition in 1976 when the BR electrification scheme from Hertford North and Welwyn Garden City to Moorgate (authorized in 1971) began operating. The Northern City Line was closed in 1975 for refurbishment to BR standards and a substitute coach service operated. A BR shuttle from Drayton Park to Old Street opened on 16th August 1976, with the full service from Finsbury Park and the BR suburban lines to Moorgate from 8th November. At King's Cross the Midland electrification scheme (in service from July 1983) caused the construction of a new subway from the Piccadilly Line to the Midland City (now Thameslink) station, and a link was also made from the subway to the Victoria Line, which improved railway interchanges and provided a street access from a new surface building in Pentonville Road.

A serious fire occurred at Oxford Circus on 23rd November

1984, when a small fire developed in a passage hoarded off for contractors' use and then spread behind and along the false ceiling of the northbound platform. Although no-one was killed a huge amount of destruction resulted, a number of people were taken to hospital and the Victoria Line service was suspended for over three weeks between Victoria and Warren Street. Temporary finishings were provided on the northbound platform and it was nearly two years before permanent ones were completed, in a style different from other platforms on the line but in keeping with modernization of the Bakerloo Line platforms (the motifs on the southbound platform were also altered to match).

At Blackhorse Road British Rail moved its platforms closer to the Victoria Line station and a much improved interchange resulted, the Victoria Line ticket office also selling BR tickets. The remaining stations have stayed largely unchanged since the line opened. Finsbury Park station has not changed much at platform level since the Victoria Line arrived, but BR has recently completed a major modernization of its street level frontage, including the final obliteration of traces of the partly-built Northern City Line high-level platforms which were an eyesore for many years. The Wells Terrace entrance to the station had been rebuilt by LT in the early 1970s. At Green Park new seat motifs were introduced at about the time the Jubilee Line opened in 1979.

To increase the number of trains available several 1972 Mk I stock trains rendered surplus on the Northern Line have been transferred to the Victoria Line. These 7-car trains are being split up and modified, and the cars are being pooled with 1967 stock cars to create additional units. Although the 1972 stock is compatible with the 1967 stock it is not equipped with the auto drive equipment and cannot be used on the extreme ends of trains. On the subject of rolling stock it is worth observing that the closure of the central overhaul facilities at Acton Works has recently transferred heavy overhaul to Northumberland Park where four additional covered sidings were recently commissioned.

The Victoria Line is now stretched to capacity at many times of the day, reflecting the recent upsurge of traffic on the Underground as a whole. It is doubtful if any substantial improvements to passenger flow can be made without inordinate expenditure, though several 'pinch points' are being examined, especially at Victoria which can barely cope with passenger numbers during the rush hours. More faith is therefore being pinned on the provision of new tube railways in central London, which are being studied at the moment, to ease the most heavily overcrowded sections of line and the most congested stations – including Victoria. But this is where we came in.